DEAR SANTA
A Musical "Tweet" for Christ...

by John Jacobson & Mac Huff

Table of Contents

3

Musical Performance Rights

HAL•LEONARD®
CORPORATION
7777 W. BLUEMOUND RD. P.O. BOX 13819 MILWAUKEE, WI 53213

Visit Hal Leonard Online at
www.halleonard.com

1 OPENING

(The musical opens with a dark stage. You hear someone punching the numbers on a telephone and then the telephone rings. An automated operator is heard.)

Operator's Voice: Happy Holidays! Welcome to the "Ask Santa" hotline. Press 1 for Santa's workshop; 2 for the reindeer barn; 3 for Elf Chat; 4 to check your naughty or nice status; 5 for returns; 6 to order your own copy of the Mrs. Claus Candy and Cookbook available only here at the North Pole Hotline. Press 7 to learn how to follow our Tweets; 8 to text; 9 to friend us on Facebook or 0 to return to the main menu.

(A beep is heard as if someone pushed one button on their phone.)

Operator's Voice: We're sorry. All of our lines are busy at the moment. Your call will be answered in the order in which it was received. There are 9 million four hundred and forty-seven callers before you. We value your call so, while you wait, please enjoy this cheerful holiday music …

SONG 1: I've Got a List

1. I've Got a List

Words and Music by
JOHN JACOBSON and MAC HUFF
Arranged by MAC HUFF

With joyful holiday spirit (♩ = 105)

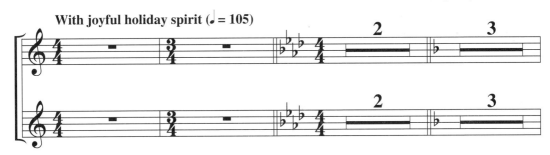

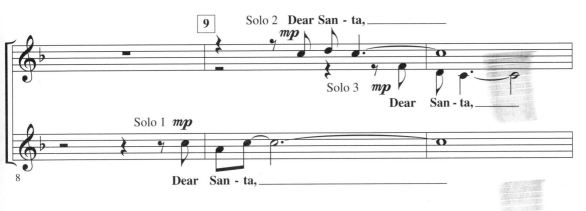

Dear Santa   3

got to set___ him right,
must com - mun - i - cate, } 'cause I've got a list.

Yeah, I've got a list.___ I I

Part I
"friend - ed" him___ on Face - book. I read ev - 'ry twit - ter too.

Part II
Oo___

We're linked to - geth - er for - ev - er, so I

Oo___ so I

know that he'll come through. My

know that he'll come through. My

51 *All*

list is short___ be - cause I'm not the sort___ to go

53 ask for ev - 'ry - thing.___ I've al - ways tried___ to be

56 sat - is - fied___ with an - y - thing you bring.___ We know

59 *cresc.*

you're the most;___ you fly from coast to coast.___ Dear San - ta,

f

61 won't you read___ my post, 'cause I've got a list.

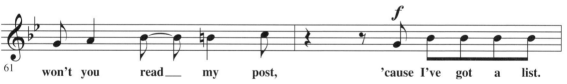

63 Yeah, I've got a list.___

Molly: *mp* 67

66 Now San - ta knows___ my sta - tus and he

checked it once_ then twice._ But up there in_____ the strat-o-sphere,_ can he see that I've been nice?

cresc.

Part II Dear

Part I Dear San - ta, Dear San - ta.__

San - ta,_____ Dear San - ta,__ Dear

Dear San - ta,

San - ta,_____ Dear San - ta._____

82 *f*

____ My list is short_ be-cause I'm not the sort_ to go

ask for ev-'ry - thing.__ I've al-ways tried_ to be

sat - is - fied_ with an - y - thing you bring.__ We know

SCENE 1

(Super Mom is being overworked and stretched to her limits with all of her responsibilities. She tries to maintain, but she's about to snap.)

Child 1: Mom, have you seen my red sweater? I left it right on this chair last week.

Mom: It's in your dresser, dear, right where it belongs.

Child 2: Mom, did you pack my lunch for the field trip today?

Mom: Yes, it's already in the refrigerator.

Child 3: Mom, I need a costume for the Christmas Play.

Mom: Yes, dear.

Child 4: Mom, I need a ride home from school.

Mom: Yes, dear.

Child 5: Mom, I told my teacher that you would chaperone the trip to the Capitol with my whole class.

Mom: Yes, dear.

Dad: Don't forget the PTA meeting tonight.

All the children and dad start talking to mom at the same time, asking her for things and reminding her of things they need her to do.

Mom: Ahhhhhhhh!!!!

(She sits down at her computer and starts typing feverishly and talking out loud. She gets progressively more worked up.)

Mom: Dear Santa, I'm keeping this short because I don't have much time. If you're reading your emails while you're on the road or in the sky, I hope you'll notice mine. I'm sending you a link to some travel sites I know. We need a vacation and we need it bad! Dear Santa! We've got to get away!

SONG 2: Getting Away for Christmas

2. Getting Away for Christmas

Words and Music by
JOHN JACOBSON and MAC HUFF
Arranged by MAC HUFF

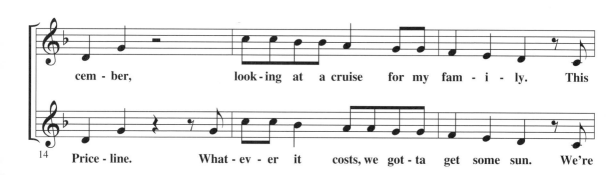

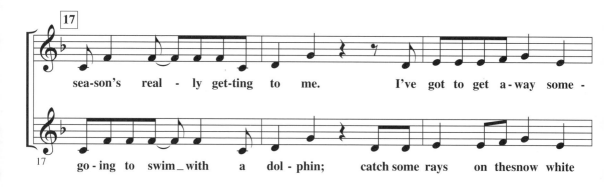

how! I'm trad-ing my miles___ and we'll head to the Isles,___ feel the

sand. I'll call Tri-ple A_____ 'cause we're not gon-na stay._ Won't come

trop - i - cal breez - es right now. We're get-ting a - way_

home 'til we're toned_____ and tan. We're get-ting a - way _

for Christ - mas. Hey, San - ta, what do you say?_

We're get - ting a - way_____ for Christ - mas.

Come on, San - ta, take us a - way._ There'll be no mis - tle - toe_

_ and hol - ly, we'll be flat on a beach_ in Ba - li,

and we'll be get-ting a - way,_ get-ting a - way_ for

Christ - mas._ The

SCENE 2

(Mom is brought back to reality.)

Dad: Honey, have you seen my white shirt?

(She buries her head in her hands.)

(Dad is looking through his closet or a chest of drawers and pulling out ridiculous ties, all gifts from past Christmases.)

Dad: *(goes over to the typewriter and starts typing aggressively; he either speaks out loud as he types or his voice from offstage is speaking what he is typing)* Dear Santa, I don't care how busy you are, you **have** to listen to me!

(He rips the paper out of the typewriter.)

Dad: *(chagrined)* I can't talk to Santa that way.

(He loads another piece of paper. He speaks or his voice is heard from offstage as he starts typing again. He speaks more politely this time.)

Dad: Dear Santa … kind sir, *(types again)*
I know that I haven't written to you since I was nine or ten years old. I'm sure you have more important things to do than listen to requests from middle-aged men …*(pauses and uses some whiteout to correct his mistake, then continues)* … from **not-quite** middle-aged men like me, but I have a simple request I hope you will take in the spirit that it's intended.

SONG 3: Anything But a Tie

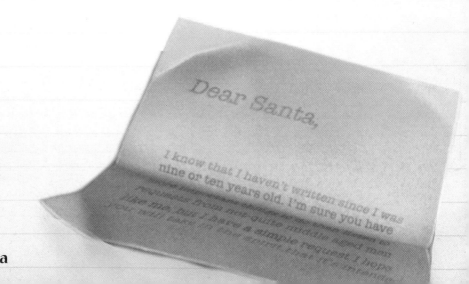

3. Anything But a Tie

Words and Music by
JOHN JACOBSON and MAC HUFF
Arranged by MAC HUFF

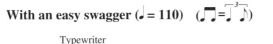

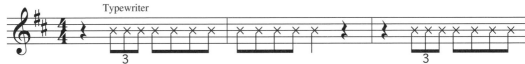

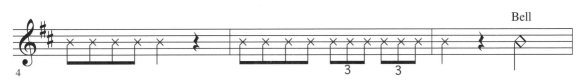

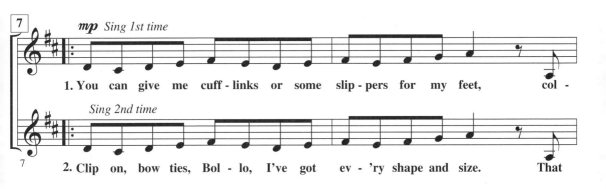

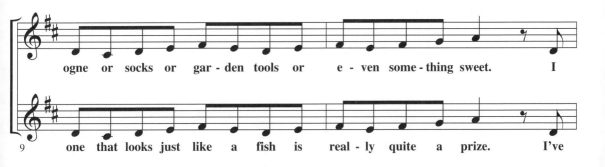

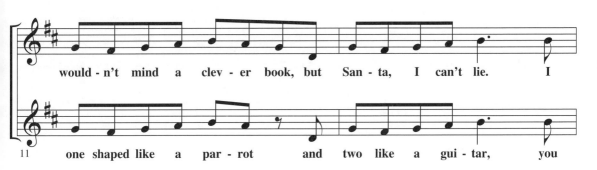

SCENE 3

(Axel, the big brother and several friends arrive home from college.)

Axel: Hey Mom, Dad! Everyone! I'm home! *(no answer)* Hello!! I'm home from college for the holidays!! Where's my greeting committee? *(gets an idea)* Oh, I know …

Axel: *(texting and talking out loud)* Mom, Dad. Flunked out of college. In the living room!

(Mom and Dad burst onto the stage.)

Dad: What? You flunked out of college?!

Mom: Oh, dear! What happened?

Axel: No, I didn't flunk out of college. I just needed to get some attention.

Dad: How did you get here so fast?

Axel: I hitchhiked.

Mom and Dad: You hitchhiked?!

Axel: What was I supposed to do? I don't have any wheels, you know. By the way, did you get my text with my Christmas list on it?

Mom: Yes, son, we did, but don't you think you're a little young for a brand new Ferrari Enzo?

Dad: What's that? A pet?

Axel: It's a hot car, Dad.

Dad: Hmmm.

Axel: You're probably right, Mom, but I know I'm going to get a car this year for sure.

Dad: Oh, really? How do you know that?

Axel: I texted my list to Santa. I said …

SONG 4: I Need Some Wheels

4. I Need Some Wheels

Words and Music by
JOHN JACOBSON and MAC HUFF
Arranged by MAC HUFF

Dear Santa   19

'cause my bike is too slow.___ I'm on the move,___ I've got some - thing___ to prove.___ San - ta, here is the deal, I need___ some wheels!_____

Axel: Mom! Dad! You never know. I might become a famous NASCAR racer. Can't you just hear it? *(pretending to be an announcer)* "And lining up on the inside post here at Talladega Super Speedway is big brother Axel in his brand new, fully-loaded Ford Fusion, courtesy of his loving parents and Santa Claus himself!"

Little Brother Joey: *(rolling his eyes)* Oh, brother!

Axel: "The crowd is going wild as big brother roars into the pit stop, where he is met by his ever-supportive parents ready to change the tires, fill the tank, and send him back out on the track. He shifts into first gear, second, third! He revs up the engine on his powerful, yet totally reasonable Christmas gift. 120! 130! 140! He rounds the corner at 170 miles an hour! Never before in the history of NASCAR has there been such a display of skill, talent and overall awesomeness! All because big brother finally got the wheels he so long deserved!
(Axel looks hopefully at his parents . . .)

Parents: *(shake heads)* Not gonna happen!
Joey: Nice try.

I see you up___ there___ in your fly - ing mag - ic sleigh.___

Run - ers are cool, but some wheels would make my day.__

___ I'm on my way___ to the ver - y top.___ So

66 San - ta, please_ don't make_ me stop. I'll take an - y au - to - mo - bile,

69 I need some wheels!_

74 *f* I need wheels;_ I've got plac - es to go._

78 I need wheels,_ 'cause my bike is too slow._

82 I'm on the move;_ I've got some - thing_ to prove.

85 _ San - ta, here is the deal, I need_ some wheels!_

88 _ I need_ some wheels!_

91 I need some wheels!_

SCENE 4

Linda: Hey, Joey. What's up?

Joey: Well, I'm trying to get Santa's attention by getting as many friends as possible on Facebook.

Linda: I'm not sure Santa is too impressed by that kind of thing.

Joey: Well, I've also been writing back and forth to a couple of elves on Elf Chat, trying to make sure that Santa gets my Christmas list in time for Christmas.

Linda: Elf Chat?

Joey: Yeah. It's a new service they offer on the North Pole website, but I don't get it.

Linda: What do you mean?

Joey: Well, I keep sending in my list and all they do is send me a link to one website.

Linda: What website is it?

Joey: *(reading slowly)* It's called the A S P C A!

Linda: ASPCA! Well, what did you ask for?

SONG 5: A Puppy for Christmas

5. A Puppy for Christmas

Words and Music by
JOHN JACOBSON and MAC HUFF
Arranged by MAC HUFF

Easy country swing (♩ = 105)

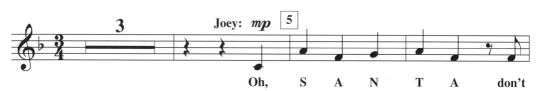

Oh, S A N T A don't

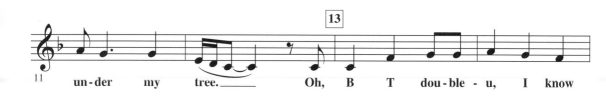

L O L at me, but I want some-thing spe-cial

un-der my tree. Oh, B T dou-ble-u, I know

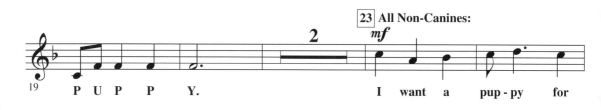

you'll real-ly try. All I want for Christ-mas is a

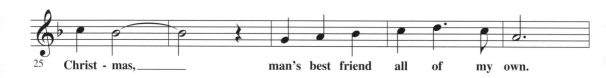

P U P P Y. I want a pup-py for

Christ-mas, man's best friend all of my own.

To love and to care for and al - ways be there for,

that's all I want for Christ - mas._____

Puppies: *mp* 41 *(opt. howl)*

Oh, give me a hoooome where a pup - py can

(opt. howl)

rooooooam, with a slip - per or two I can chew._____ I

49

won't be a pest. I will give it my best. San - ta

Claus, we are all beg - ging you._____

58 *mf*

I want a home for Christ - mas;_____ a

62 place I can call my own._____ To

66 love and to care for, and al - ways be there for;

70 that's all I want for Christ - mas._____

Non-Canines: _f_ 76

Oh, S A N T A, don't L O L at

Puppies: _f_

(opt. howl)

75 Oh, give me a hoooome where a pup - py can

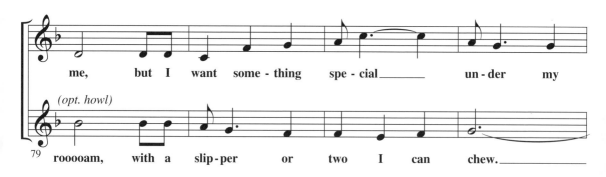

me, but I want some - thing spe - cial_____ un - der my

(opt. howl)

79 rooooam, with a slip - per or two I can chew._____

love and to care for and al - ways be there for,

love and to care for, and al - ways be there for,

that's all I want, yes, that's all I want,

that's all I want, yes, that's all I want,

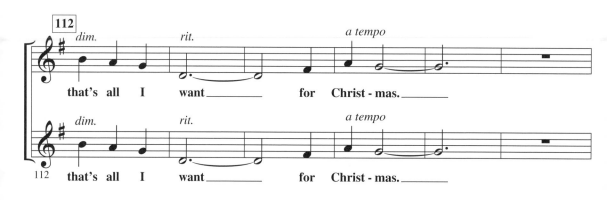

that's all I want_____ for Christ - mas._____

that's all I want_____ for Christ - mas._____

That's all I want._____

Oh, give me a home._____

SCENE 5

(Grandma and Grandpa enter in their brand new matching sweat suits and tennis shoes. There are still puppies all over the stage.)

Grandma: Well, that was a real nice walk in the mall, Grandpa Fred.

Grandpa: Yeah, Grandma Eunice; really got my heart rate going.

(They look around and see all the puppies.)

Puppies: *(all start begging with ad libs)* "Please take me home!" "Come on, Grandma!" "Take me home for Christmas!" "Look how cute I am" … etc.

Grandma: *(to the puppies)* Anyone want to go for a W-A-L-K?

Grandpa: *(takes out a rolled-up newspaper)* Here ... fetch!! *(He tosses the paper off to one side of the stage and all of the puppies chase after it, barking, to exit.)*

Grandma: You know, Grandpa Fred, I'm tired of going to that mall and walking around in circles everyday to get my exercise.

Grandpa: Me too, Eunice. There's got to be a more exciting way to workout than that.

Grandma: *(gets an idea)* I know! Let's ask Santa to bring one of those new Dance Revolution machines we saw at the arcade!

Grandpa: That's a great idea, Ma! Oh...but it's too late to send a letter to Santa now. It's only a few days until Christmas. Our letter will never get there.

(They pause and think, scratching their heads, etc.)

Grandma: I know! Let's do the SKYPE thing!

Grandpa: You mean talk to Santa Claus on Skype like we do with our grand kids? Of course, that's a great idea!

Grandma: We'll never get Santa himself at this late date, but Mrs. Claus is always online these days. I think she's internet-addicted. Come on, let's give it a try.

(Grandma and Grandpa walk downstage center to a laptop computer, which they open. The computer has its back to the audience. They push a few buttons, then we hear the Skype tone.)

Grandpa: North Pole First Lady. That's her Skype name. Ring it up, Grandma! See if she'll answer.

(We hear the Skype ring. If possible Mrs. Claus would appear on a screen so that the audience could see her. If not, Mrs. Claus could be seen looking into a computer on another part of the stage. Third choice, we simply hear her voice from offstage.)

Mrs. Claus: Hello! Hello! Mrs. Claus here! Can you see me!? Can you see me now?

Grandma: Yes, Mrs. C., we can see you! You look great!

Mrs. Claus: Oh, I don't know. They say these screens add twenty pounds to your look!

Grandpa: Oh, Mrs. Claus, don't be ridiculous! You look ... well, you look like Mrs. Claus!!

Mrs. Claus: Oh, Grandpa Fred, how nice of you to say so! How are things where you are, Fred and Eunice?

Grandpa: Oh, they're just great, Mrs. C! We've had a wonderful year!

Grandma: I got a new titanium shoulder in July!

Grandpa: And I got some snap-on teeth in November! See! *(smiles to show off his teeth)*

Mrs. Claus: Beautiful! So glad to hear it! Then, Grandma and Grandpa, what can I do for you? Would you like a new puppy or maybe some new wheels for Christmas? There's still room in Santa's sleigh for a Cadillac or a snowmobile, if you want one!

Grandma: Oh no, Mrs. Claus! We don't need anything like that. We want one of those new fangled dance revolution machines we saw those young people jumping around at, down at the mall.

Grandpa: Yah, you know, the kind where the music plays and you make your feet do the moves … like this. *(does a funny dance)* We've heard it's great exercise!

Mrs. Claus: *(laughing)* Oh ho ho! You two crack me up! But are you sure that's a good idea for people your, er … age?

Grandma: Look who's talking! Mrs. C, you're like 200 years old yourself!

Mrs. Claus: Ho Ho Ho! *(suddenly concerned)* Oo, you're right. I guess I am.

Grandpa: Well, we'd like to shake a leg, if you know what I mean!

Mrs. Claus: Oh, I know *exactly* what you mean, Grandpa! If a dance revolution is what you want under your Christmas tree, rest assured, you can count on me!

Grandma: We knew we could, Mrs. C!!

Mrs. Claus: Ho Ho Ho! Now, go shake a leg or two, but don't overdo it, and have a wonderful Christmas and a happy new year! Bye! Goodbye!

(Mrs. Claus goes off and song begins.)

SONG 6: Holiday Dance Revolution

6. Holiday Dance Revolution

Words and Music by
JOHN JACOBSON and MAC HUFF
Arranged by MAC HUFF

32   **Dear Santa**

Hol - i - day Dance rev - o - lu - tion;____ groove to a hol - i - day song.__

28 ____ Bring your friends__ and neigh - bors and

31 par - ty,_____ par - ty all night long.____

Grandpa: Come on, Eunice! Pull up your stockings!
Let's rock and roll!

'50s Rock *(same tempo)*

3   4

34

41 *f*

Up on the house - top rein - deer pause,_ out jumps good old

44 San - ta Claus._ Down through the chim - ney with lots of toys;_

49

47 all for the lit - tle ones, Christ - mas joys._ Ho ho ho,

50 go!   Ho ho ho, go!

54 Up on the house - top click, click, click,_

57 down through the chim - ney with good Saint Nick!

Grandma: Come on, Grandpa Fred! Let's do another one!
(like a chant as she dances) Step left! Step right! We can dance all day and night!

Grandpa: Great! What kind of music do you want next, Grandma?

Grandma: Oh, Grandpa! You know what I like!

Grandpa: *(worried)* Oh, Ma! Last time we got funky with it,
I was in my Lazy Boy for six weeks!!

Grandma: Come on, Fred!
Let's boogie!!

Grandpa: Oh well,
'tis the season!

64 Funk (♩ = 115)

f

Ow!

7

Hey!

74
Jol - ly Old Saint Nich - o - las, _ lean your ear this way.

78
Don't you tell a sin - gle soul what I'm going to say. _

82
Christ - mas Eve is com - ing soon. _ Now you dear old man,

86
whis - per what you'll bring to me. Tell me if _____ you

90
can. Tell ___ me if you can.

Grandpa: *(chanting and dancing)*
Hop left. Right skip! Oops! I think I broke a hip!

2

2

94

Grandma: Come on, kids! We're cookin' now!

Kid 1: That's not the kind of cookin' I expected from my grandma!
Kid 2: What's gotten into Grandma and Grandpa?
Kid 3: I think they've been watching too much You Tube!
Kid 4: We're going to have to put some restrictions on their computer!

Grandpa: Come on, kids! Let's dance!

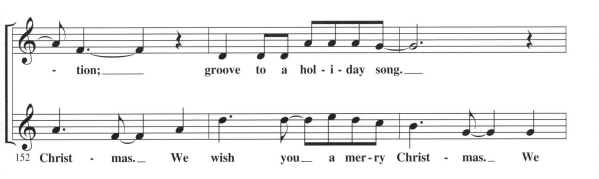

-tion;_____ groove to a hol-i-day song.___

Christ - mas.___ We wish you___ a mer-ry Christ - mas.___ We

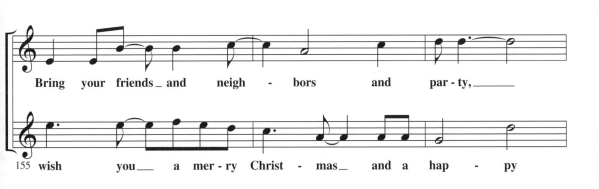

Bring your friends___ and neigh - bors and par-ty,_____

wish you___ a mer-ry Christ - mas___ and a hap - py

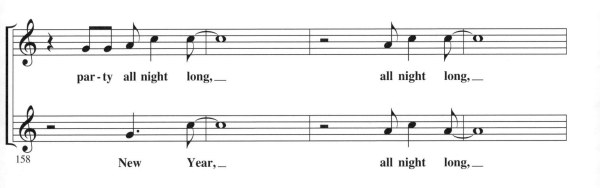

par-ty all night long, ___ all night long, ___

New Year,___ all night long,___

All **ff**

all night long._____ Let's Dance!

all night long._____

SCENE 6

(Little girl Molly is sitting in the middle of the stage writing a letter.)

Grandma: Hi, Molly. How did you like our dance?

Molly: It was awesome, Grandma and Grandpa!

Grandpa: Yeah, I know.

Grandma: So Molly, what are you doing?

Molly: Oh, I've been doing a lot of thinking, and now I'm ready to write my letter to Santa Claus.

Grandpa: You're **writing** him a letter? You mean, like with paper and pen?

Grandma: How quaint. You know Skyping would be a lot faster.

(Axel, Linda, Joey, a puppy or two, and Mom and Dad enter quickly.)

Axel: Molly, what are you doing? Don't you know it would be better just to text Santa?

Joey: Or go through Elf Chat?

Mother: Or Facebook?

Father: Or e-mail?

Puppy: Woof!

Molly: Yes, I suppose it would be faster to use one of those modern methods to get to Santa Claus, but I guess I just like the old-fashioned way. In fact, I guess I just like an old-fashioned Christmas all around.

All : Huh?

Puppy: *(half spoken, half barked)* Me too.

Molly: Oh, don't get me wrong. I think all of those wonderful new gadgets are fantastic and I'll probably get back in the mix right after New Years. But, I think Christmas ought to be a time when we all slow down, instead of speed up … look around us and celebrate the wonderful things in our lives.

Mother: You mean like family?

Axel: ... and friends?

Joey: … brothers and sisters?

Grandma: … grandmas?

Grandpa: … and grandpas?

Puppy: Puppies? *(They all look at him.)* I mean, Woof!

Molly: Exactly! So I'm writing Santa a letter and if it doesn't get there before Christmas, it's okay, because it's mostly a thank you note anyway, just saying thanks for helping to spread joy all around the world each year at Christmas time.

Puppy: *(in puppy talk)* Nice!

Linda: Well, knock yourself out! None of the rest of us have been able to get through to Santa … maybe you can.

Molly: *(starting to write her letter, speaking in rhyme)*
Dear Santa, How are you? I am fine.
I hope that your Christmas is joyful and jolly.
I know I can count on you. It's me, Molly.
With shopping and parties, we rush in and out.
I'm worried we forget what the season's all about.

Grandma: Well, what's on your list, Molly? We'd all like to know.

SONG 7: Sincerely, Christmas

7. Sincerely, Christmas

Words and Music by
JOHN JACOBSON and MAC HUFF
Arranged by MAC HUFF

Gently, with a lilt (♩ = 108)

Molly: *p*

Har - mo - ny and hap - pi - ness for ev - 'ry liv - ing thing;

chil - dren spread - ing joy and love with car - ols that they sing;

peo - ple show - ing that they care and spread - ing Christ - mas cheer;

that's what I dream of sin - cere - ly._____

All **mp**

May - be we could look a - round and no - tice folks in need.
All I want is ev - 'ry - one to love and do what's right;

Ev - 'ry - one could find a way to do a kind - ly deed.
pray for peace and har - mo - ny up - on this si - lent night;

No one has to be a - lone or live a life in fear;
fam - i - lies to - geth - er now from far and some from near;

One more thing,   dear San-ta Claus,   for what-ev-er it is worth,   I

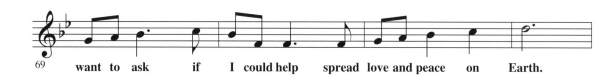

want to ask   if   I could help   spread love and peace   on   Earth.

I know it's   a   lot to ask   but, dear San-ta   dear,

78   **Moving Ahead**

that's what   I dream of,   that's what   I long for,   that is what   I

wish   for   sin-cere-ly_____   this   Christ-mas._____

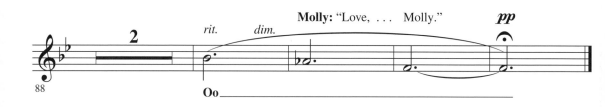

Molly: "Love, . . . Molly."

Oo_____

SCENE 7

(The sound of sleigh bells is heard, along with a lot of "Ho Ho Ho-ing.")

All: It's Santa!!

Santa: *(enters and ad libs)* Ho Ho Ho! Merry Christmas, everybody! Ho Ho Ho!

(The cast also ad libs "Hi Santa!" "Merry Christmas, Santa!" "We love you, Santa!" etc.)

Santa: Ho Ho Ho! I'm so happy to see all of you.

Father: But Santa, shouldn't you be busy getting ready for your annual trip around the world?

(These next five lines can all be said at about the same time … overloading Santa with requests and reminders.)

Mother: Yes, Santa and by the way, did you get my e-mail about a little get-away vacation this year?

Father: And mine … remember *(mouths the words and does a slicing motion by his neck)* No ties!

Axel: Did you hear I got my driver's license, Santa? Hint hint!

Joey: And I sent you a link to the ASPCA!

Puppy: Woof!

Santa: Oh, yes! I got all of your e-mails and tweets, Facebook messages and texts. I'm sure all of you will be very happy come Christmas morning. Ho Ho Ho! But I really came here to see a little girl named Molly. You see, I just got her beautiful letter this morning.

Molly: Wow! That was fast!

Santa: Molly, I want to thank you for reminding me and everybody else here today what Christmas is all about.

Grandpa: I guess we have all been a little selfish with our Christmas lists.

Grandma: Yes, I guess we don't really *need* a dance revolution machine to cut a rug or two.

Santa: Ho Ho Ho! Don't be silly and don't be sad. Christmas is a season for giving **and** receiving! I think it's fun to do both! I just love the new mittens Mrs. Claus made for me. *(shows his mittens)* It's fun to get a gift from someone you love and someone who put some real thought and effort into that special gift for you!

Molly: But it's about giving too, isn't it, Santa?

Santa: That's right, Molly! Thank you for reminding us all that Christmas is a time for sharing, for reaching out and giving your best to make sure all are happy, healthy and enjoying peace on Earth, Goodwill to all!

Molly: Sincerely!

SONG: Finale Reprise

8. Finale Reprise

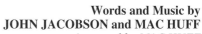

Words and Music by
JOHN JACOBSON and MAC HUFF
Arranged by MAC HUFF

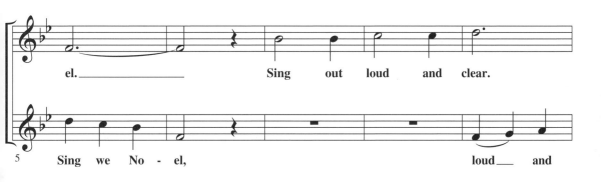

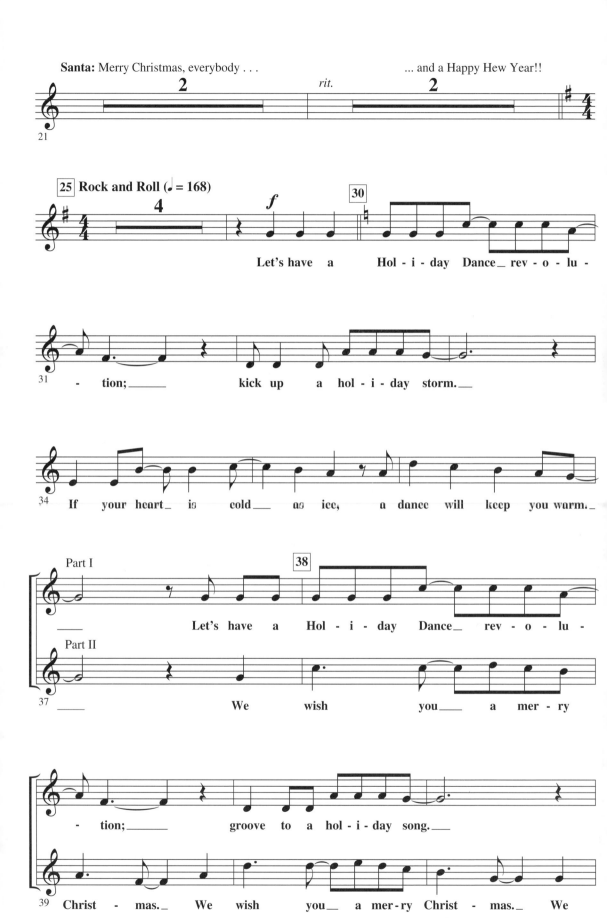

Bring your friends and neigh - bors and

wish you a mer - ry Christ - mas and a

par - ty, party all night long,

hap - py New Year,

all night long, all night long.

all night long, all night long.

ff

Mer - ry Christ-mas!

ff

Mer - ry Christ-mas!

Dear Santa 47